D1411985

**HEINEMANN
STATE STUDIES**

All Around
New Jersey

Mark Stewart

Heinemann Library
Chicago, Illinois

Designed by Heinemann Library
Page layout by Wilkinson Design
Printed and bound in the United States by
    Lake Book Manufacturing, Inc.

08 07 06 05 04
10 9 8 7 6 5 4 3 2 1

**Library of Congress
Cataloging-in-Publication Data**

Stewart, Mark, 1960-
   All around New Jersey : regions and resources /
Mark Stewart.   p. cm. -- (State studies)
Summary: Provides an overview of New Jersey's
geographic regions, including their resources,
landforms, industries, climate, and transportation.
Includes bibliographical references and index.
   ISBN 1-4034-0672-3 (hc : library binding) -- ISBN
1-4034-2682-1 (pb) 1. New Jersey--Description
and travel--Juvenile literature. 2. New Jersey--
Geography--Juvenile literature. 3. Regionalism--
New Jersey--Juvenile literature. 4. New Jersey--His-
tory, Local--Juvenile literature. [1. New Jersey--
Geography. 2. Regionalism--New Jersey.] I. Title. II.
Series. F134.3.S754 2003
   917.49--dc21

2003010354

Acknowledgments

The author and publishers are grateful to the
following for permission to reproduce copyright
material:

Cover photographs by (main) Najlah Feanny/
Corbis SABA; (row, L-R) Kelly-Mooney
Photography, Kelly-Mooney Photography, Mark
Peterson/Corbis SABA, Bob Krist/Corbis

Title page (L-R) Lee Snider/Corbis, David
Muench/Corbis, George Goodwin/Color Pic, Inc.;
contents page (L-R) Carol Kitman; Phil Degginger/
Color Pic, Inc.; pp. 4, 10b, 14, 19t, 23, 39, 42, 44
Kelly-Mooney Photography; p. 7 Ed Eckstein/
Corbis; pp. 10t, 16b, 33 Phil Degginger/Color Pic,
Inc.; p. 12 George Goodwin/Color Pic, Inc.; p. 15
David Muench/Corbis; p. 16t Raymond Gehman/
Corbis; p. 17 George McNish/Star Ledger/AP Wide
World Photos; p. 19b E. R. Degginger/Color Pic,
Inc.; pp. 20, 24, 30b, 43 Michael S. Yamashita;
pp. 21, 26t, 41 Walter Choroszewski Photography;
pp. 25, 30t, 36 Lee Snider/Corbis; p. 26b Daniel
Hulshizer/AP Wide World Photos; p. 27 Charles E.
Rotkin/Corbis; pp. 28, 32, 38t, 40b Hector
Emmanuel/Heinemann Library; p. 29 Sheldan
Collins/Corbis; p. 31 Carol Kitman; p. 34 Kelly-
Mooney Photography/Corbis; p. 38b Bettmann/
Corbis; p. 40t Richard T. Nowitz/Corbis

Photo research by John Klein

Special thanks to expert reader Chad Leinaweaver,
the Director for the Library at The New Jersey
Historical Society, for his help in the preparation
of this book.

Every effort has been made to contact copyright
holders of any material reproduced in this book.
Any omissions will be rectified in subsequent
printings if notice is given to the publisher.

Some words are shown in bold, **like this.**
You can find out what they mean by looking
in the glossary.

Contents

New Jersey's Geography and Resources

New Jersey has more people for its size than any other state. It is the most **densely** populated state. It leads the nation in many other areas, too. Its millions of people live in different regions and work in different **industries.** New Jersey has areas of wilderness, a rich history, and many places of interest.

New Jersey is located on the east coast of the United States. It is bordered by New York to the north, and New York City sits on its eastern and northern border at Jersey City. Two states border New Jersey on the west— Pennsylvania and Delaware. Delaware Bay lies between the states of New Jersey and Delaware, and the Delaware River separates New Jersey from Pennsylvania and Delaware. The Atlantic Ocean lies to the east of New Jersey. New Jersey is a **peninsula.**

New Jersey's coastline along the Atlantic Ocean is 130 miles long.

New Jersey Topography

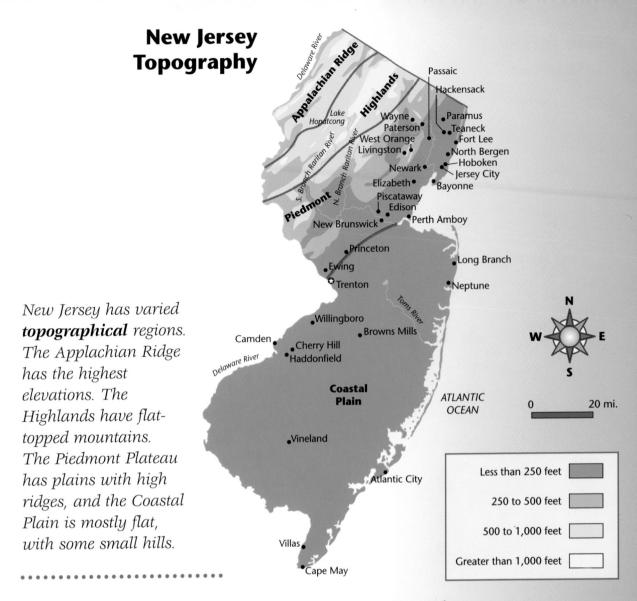

New Jersey has varied **topographical** regions. The Applachian Ridge has the highest elevations. The Highlands have flat-topped mountains. The Piedmont Plateau has plains with high ridges, and the Coastal Plain is mostly flat, with some small hills.

New Jersey is made up of four major regions: the Appalachian Ridge, the Highlands, Piedmont Plateau, and Coastal Plain. The state's treasures within each of these regions are both natural and **artificial.**

CLIMATE

As you travel south in New Jersey, you find warmer temperatures than in the northern part of the state. In the month of July temperatures average about 70°F in the north and 75°F in the south. January temperatures average 34°F in the south and 30°F in the north. Average annual precipitation ranges from 40 inches on the south-eastern coast to about 50 inches in the north-central part of the state. New Jersey has a **temperate climate.**

New Jersey Resources

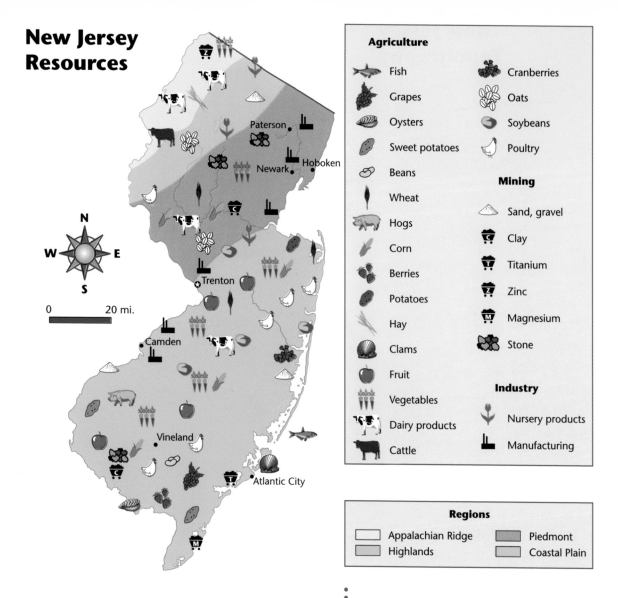

Agriculture

- Fish
- Grapes
- Oysters
- Sweet potatoes
- Beans
- Wheat
- Hogs
- Corn
- Berries
- Potatoes
- Hay
- Clams
- Fruit
- Vegetables
- Dairy products
- Cattle
- Cranberries
- Oats
- Soybeans
- Poultry

Mining

- Sand, gravel
- Clay
- Titanium
- Zinc
- Magnesium
- Stone

Industry

- Nursery products
- Manufacturing

Regions

- Appalachian Ridge
- Highlands
- Piedmont
- Coastal Plain

New Jersey has a wide range of natural and human-made resources. Agriculture, mining, and manufacturing are three of New Jersey's largest industries.

NATURAL RESOURCES

Natural resources are materials found in nature that are useful to people. Valuable natural resources in New Jersey include forests, water, land, and minerals, which provide citizens with many opportunities for jobs.

Only four other states are smaller in size than New Jersey, which covers a total area of about 8,200 square miles. This includes over 7,400 square miles of land and about 700 square miles of water. More than 4,100 lakes and ponds and 8,600 miles of rivers and streams make up the water areas of New Jersey. The longest rivers in the state are the Hudson and the Delaware. The Atlantic Ocean is also a key water resource for the state.

Landforms in New Jersey range from high mountains to low plains. The land is rich in minerals, such as limestone, granite, and basalt. Nearly two-fifths of the state is covered with forests, while almost one-fifth of its land area is used for farming. Much of the rest of New Jersey is made up of developed **urban** or **suburban** areas, where people live and work.

More than 80 varieties of fruits, vegetables, and other agriculture are produced by the Garden State, as New Jersey is sometimes called. There are over 9,000 farms in New Jersey. Their biggest crops are nursery and greenhouse products, followed by vegetables and fruit. The state's dairy and poultry **industries** are also important. New Jersey's farmland has the highest dollar value of any farmland in the United States.

INDUSTRY

New Jersey may be one of the smallest states in the nation, but it has the ninth biggest **economy.** Its **gross state product** is $363 billion. New Jersey has such a

*Fifteen of the twenty largest **pharmaceutical** companies in the world have major facilities in New Jersey.*

The New Jersey Economy

Gross State Product in 2001 (in dollars)

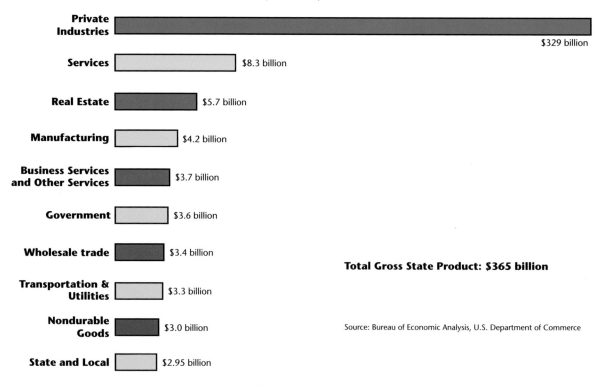

Private Industries	$329 billion
Services	$8.3 billion
Real Estate	$5.7 billion
Manufacturing	$4.2 billion
Business Services and Other Services	$3.7 billion
Government	$3.6 billion
Wholesale trade	$3.4 billion
Transportation & Utilities	$3.3 billion
Nondurable Goods	$3.0 billion
State and Local	$2.95 billion

Total Gross State Product: $365 billion

Source: Bureau of Economic Analysis, U.S. Department of Commerce

The money earned by private industries makes up the largest share of New Jersey's gross state product. Private companies do not sell stock to the public.

large **gross state product** because it uses its **natural resources** to support major **industries.**

New Jersey is known for its chemicals and **pharmaceutical** products. Electronic equipment, processed food, machinery, and a large range of other products are made in New Jersey. **High-tech** and medical research companies have grown in more recent years. Manufacturing accounts for about one-fifth of New Jersey's gross state product.

Where there are people, there are services to make their lives easier. Of all of New Jersey's industries, the service industry is the biggest. It includes hotels, restaurants, and health services. Businesses that provide services for **recreation,** such as movie theaters, also are in the service industry. Overall, services represent almost one-quarter of New Jersey's **economy.**

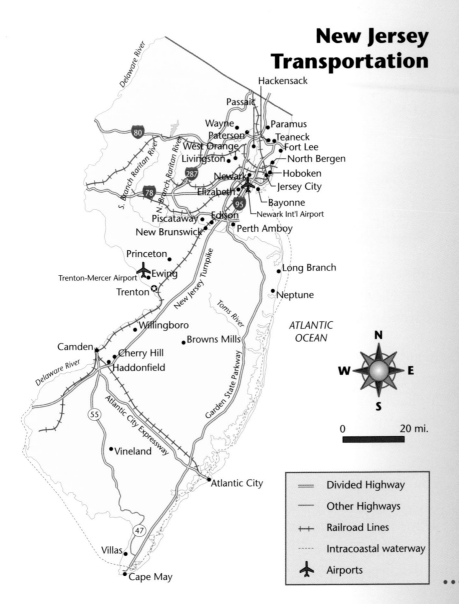

New Jersey Transportation

Delaware River

Hackensack

Passaic

Wayne
Paramus
Paterson
Teaneck
West Orange
Fort Lee
Livingston
North Bergen

80

287

Newark
Hoboken
Jersey City
Elizabeth

78

95

Bayonne
Edison
Newark Int'l Airport
Piscataway
New Brunswick
Perth Amboy

S. Branch Raritan River

N. Branch Raritan River

Princeton

Long Branch

Trenton-Mercer Airport
Ewing
Trenton

New Jersey Turnpike

Neptune

Toms River

ATLANTIC
OCEAN

Willingboro

Browns Mills

Camden
Cherry Hill
Haddonfield

Delaware River

Garden State Parkway

N

W   E

S

55

Atlantic City Expressway

0   20 mi.

Vineland

Atlantic City

| Divided Highway |
| Other Highways |
| Railroad Lines |
| Intracoastal waterway |
| Airports |

47

Villas

Cape May

Many people use New Jersey's roads, airports, railroads, and waterways. For example, the Garden State Parkway carries well over a million vehicles per day. One out of every five vehicles is from out-of-state.

TRANSPORTATION AND TOURISM

Anyone traveling by car in New Jersey knows that its road system is one of the best in the United States. As the country's most **densely** populated state, New Jersey's roads are what keeps things moving. New Jersey links other big industrial centers in the northeastern United States with southern and western areas of the country. New Jersey has more than 35,000 miles of roads, including over 400 miles of interstate

The New Jersey Turnpike (I-95) is a megahighway of 6 to 12 lanes used by heavy trucks and bordered in some parts by a gray industrial landscape. This view of the state can give people the wrong idea about how New Jersey really looks.

highways. It is connected by bridges and tunnels with New York City, and has almost 1,000 miles of railroad tracks.

Besides roads, there are seaports in the cities of Newark and Elizabeth, and smaller **ports** on the Delaware River at Paulsboro, Camden, Gloucester City, and Trenton. There are also over 50 airports in New Jersey. The busiest is Newark Liberty International Airport.

Tourists come to New Jersey for its ocean **resorts,** mountains, lakes, and **scenic** areas. Many visitors to New Jersey go to Atlantic City. Its beaches, boardwalks, and casinos attract 45 million visitors each year. Others visit one or more of New Jersey's 36 state parks and 11 state forests. Other popular tourist destinations include the Liberty Science Center at Liberty State Park in

Besides the casinos, Atlantic City also offers a beach, a boardwalk, amusement rides, and plenty of food.

New Jersey Precipitation

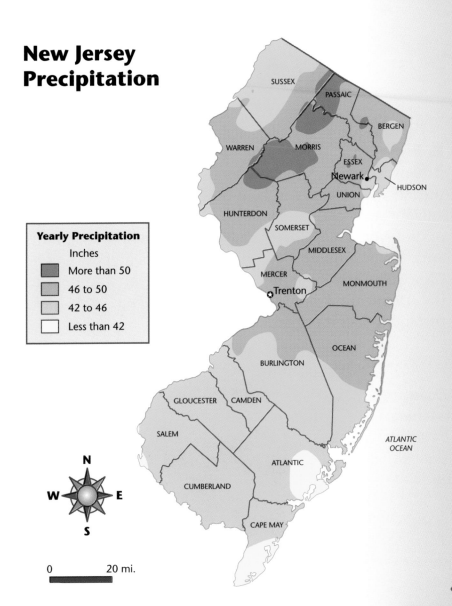

Yearly Precipitation

Inches

More than 50

46 to 50

42 to 46

Less than 42

In New Jersey, precipitation falls about 120 days out of the year. Most areas receive 25 to 30 thunderstorms per year as well.

Jersey City, Six Flags Great Adventure in Jackson, and The State Planetarium in Trenton. Tourists are important for New Jersey. They spend over $30 billion each year during their visits.

NEW JERSEY: THE GARDEN STATE

New Jersey has a lot to offer people, whether they are residents or visitors. A **thriving economy,** many solid **industries,** a **temperate climate,** and many attractions make New Jersey a great place to live, work, and play.

Appalachian Ridge

New Jersey's Appalachian Ridge region is a mix of rugged wilderness and beautiful pastureland. The most ancient exposed rocks in the state—more than 600 million years old—form the Kittatinny Mountains in this area. They contain some of New Jersey's highest points. The Delaware River flows through the area known as the Delaware Water Gap, cutting a deep, wide path through these mountains.

*The **scenic** Delaware Water Gap is situated where the Delaware River flows through the Kittatinny Mountains.*

LANDFORMS

The natural beauty of New Jersey's Appalachian Ridge makes it a popular area for tourism. There are little towns all along the Delaware River, and the state's northern corner is known for its hiking and canoeing.

The **vista** from High Point State Park, located in this region, is among the state's best. Located just north of the town of Sussex, it is a park that offers a view of three different states from a height of 1,803 feet. As its name implies, High Point is the highest point in New Jersey. To the west you can see Pennsylvania's Pocono Mountains. To the east are New York's Catskill Mountains. To the south is the patchwork of forests, farms, and homes of New Jersey's Sussex County.

Appalachian Ridge Region

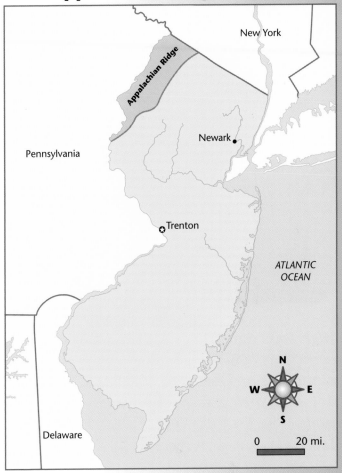

The Appalachian Ridge creases the northwest corner of New Jersey.

Sunfish Pond sits in a natural state at the crest of the Kittatinny Ridge, near Pahaquarry Township. The crystal-clear waters cover a half-mile stretch carved out by an ancient glacier. **Conservationists** consider Sunfish Pond one of the state's rare treasures, and have taken steps to prevent **recreational** activity near its shores. Boating and fishing are popular sports in other parts of the Appalachian Ridge, including Swartswood State Park, near the town of Newton, and at numerous points along the Delaware River.

High Point State Park is 14,193 acres. It is home to a number of attractions and activities, including a natural area and several hiking trails.

Tillman Ravine, near the town of Branchville, is in Stokes State Forest. Surrounded by ancient hemlocks and rhododendrum, the ravine was created by Tillman Brook as it cut down the side of the Kittatinny Mountains. **Geologists** like to study this area, because they believe that many thousands of years from now it may become a **gorge.**

A PLACE OF REFUGE

There are no big cities in the Appalachian Ridge region, which measures about 10 to 13 miles wide. The stretch of the Delaware River within the region never attracted big **industries,** and no major cities arose. Instead, people thought of it as a place of **refuge.** This may be why there are villages in the Appalachian Ridge with names such as Harmony, Tranquility, and Hope. Throughout this heavily forested region are **secluded** valleys. Although they are not **fertile** enough to support heavy farming, they make perfect grazing land for cows.

Sunfish Pond is one of the most popular hiking destinations in New Jersey.

The busiest place in the region is the town of Vernon, with a population of more than 20,000. Throughout the year, hikers wander in and out of Vernon, which is right on the Appalachian Trail. In the summer, golfers enjoy its ten golf courses. In the winter, skiers from all over the state come to the slopes at Mountain Creek.

Take a Hike

The Appalachian Trail runs unbroken through New Jersey. This is the only state in which this occurs.

There are no other large towns in this region of New Jersey. Perhaps the most popular of the smaller ones is Augusta, the location of the Sussex County Fairgrounds. This town is also the location of Skylands Park, a baseball stadium. It is home to the New Jersey Cardinals, a minor league team owned by the St. Louis Cardinals.

One of the most interesting small towns in this region is Walpack Center, which actually sits within the borders of the 70,000-acre Delaware Water Gap National **Recreation** Area. Various hikes and day trips begin from Walpack Center. It is close to Peters Valley, a craft education center that is open to the public.

Mountain Creek Ski **Resort** *is in Vernon Valley. Its 1,000-foot drop is the highest of any ski resort in the area.*

The Highlands

New Jersey's Highlands run in a diagonal band across the northwestern section of the state. The area has dramatic flat-top ridges, which include the Ramapo and Passaic Mountains. The Highlands measure eight miles across at the Delaware River, and widen gradually as they approach New Jersey's border with New York. The highest peak in the Highlands is Bearfort Mountain, at just about 1,500 feet. The Highlands include parts of Warren, Morris, Sussex, and Passaic counties.

Hikers in the Wyanokie Highlands can see the Manhattan skyline 40 miles to the south and the blue Wanaque Reservoir in the valley below.

The Highland Region of New Jersey

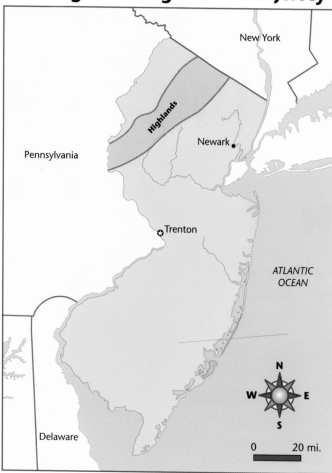

New Jersey's Highlands region has over one million acres of forests, lakes, and streams.

NATURAL RESOURCES

Many streams and rivers cut through this region, including the Musconetcong River. It begins at Lake Hopatcong and empties into the Delaware River. The rivers in the region created long, deep valleys that were home to New Jersey's native peoples. When European settlers came, they discovered these areas offered tremendous **natural resources**—including iron **ore,** zinc, and grazing land. The **landforms** of the region provided shelter and protection for the Continental Army during the American Revolution (1775–1783). Today, the valleys are filled with **suburbs,** historic sites, **quaint** towns, dairy farms, and **recreational** areas.

Another popular spot in the region is the Franklin Mine. In the mid-1800s, the discovery of zinc in this location launched a new **industry** for New Jersey. It was one of

Franklin Mine produced $500 million worth of zinc over a period of 106 years!

over 200 different minerals to be found in Franklin—many of which are quite rare, and even a few that do not occur anywhere else in the world. The mine shut down in the 1950s, but a museum and the searchable Buckwheat Dump now draw thousands of mineral collectors every year. At Buckwheat Dump, collectors can take home up to ten pounds of discarded rock from the mine.

At the northernmost end of the Highlands region, on the New York state border, there are two

*Ringwood State Park, home of the Skylands Gardens, features 5,000 **species** of flowers, plants, and trees.*

magnificent old homes—Ringwood Manor and Skylands Manor—as well as a lake with a swimming beach. The property was originally built in the mid-1700s after rich deposits of iron **ore** were discovered in the area. For well over a century, Ringwood was an important part of the state's iron **industry.**

Something Fishy

New Jersey has some of the nation's best sport fishing, but few realize that it is not limited to the Atlantic Ocean. The state stocks more than 100 lakes and streams with over a half-million trout each year. Most are raised at the Pequest Trout Hatchery, which is part of the Pequest River Wildlife Management Area in Oxford. This fascinating facility lets you see brown, rainbow, and brook trout grow from egg to "long-fry"—a process that takes about five weeks. From there the fish are moved to a holding tank, where they are kept until they are 18 months old. They are then transported and released into the lakes and rivers throughout the state. Not surprisingly, one of the best and prettiest fishing spots in New Jersey is just a few hundred yards away from the hatchery.

Piedmont Plateau

Most of New Jersey's major population areas are located in the Piedmont Plateau. This region runs from the Delaware River in the southwest to the Hudson River and the New York border in the northeast. The word *Piedmont* means "foothills." The central point of this region is Morristown. On the western edge, where the hills flatten out to the Coastal Plain, is New Jersey's state capital, Trenton. Bunched together in the eastern section of this region are cities such as Newark, Elizabeth, and Paterson.

The Piedmont Plateau is a mixture of **urban** and farmland areas. Here you can see how near the cities are to the farmlands.

Piedmont Plateau Region

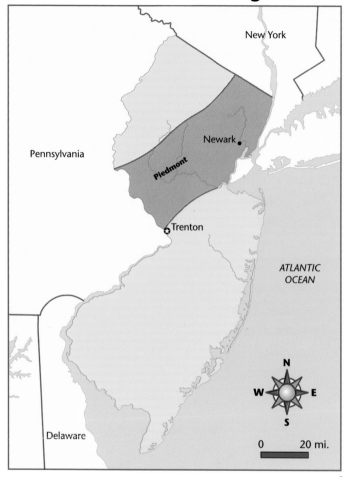

The Piedmont Plateau region begins in New Jersey and extends south all the way to Florida. It runs alongside the Appalachian Mountains.

LANDFORMS

The northern end of Hoboken marks the unofficial beginning of the Palisades, dramatic cliffs that stretch up the west side of the Hudson River right into New York state. The towns atop this ridge have good city views. Residents of towns like Weehawken, Guttenberg, and North Bergen wake up each morning to the sun rising over the New York City skyline. In the evening, the city is awash in a hundred different colors as the sun sets in the west. A **promenade** runs right up to Cliffside Park, offering an amazing **vista** of the Hudson from the Verrazano Bridge to the George Washington Bridge in historic Fort Lee.

On the western side of the Palisades is marshland known as the Meadowlands. Much of this area has been drained, providing buildable land for office and shopping complexes, as well as Giants Stadium, Continental Airlines Arena, and the Meadowlands Racetrack. The Hackensack River winds its way through this area from the **suburbs** in northern Bergen County.

What Lies Beneath

One of New Jersey's most interesting features is one no one has ever seen: the Ramapo Fault. It is located deep underground, and follows the rough line that divides the Highlands from the Piedmont Plateau. **Geologists** estimate that it is a billion years old, and was extremely active around 200 million years ago. That is not to say it is **dormant**—every few years residents of Bergen, Morris, and Somerset counties feel a little reminder of what lies beneath. The last big earthquake along the fault occurred in 1886.

During the 1800s, as New York City grew, stone was needed to pave its streets. For many years, this material was stripped from the face of New Jersey's Palisades and ferried across the Hudson River. Angered by the destruction of this natural wonder, more than 300 members of New Jersey's Federation of Women's Clubs marched on the State House in Trenton to protest. At first, the protests had little effect. The stone companies paid state politicians to keep them from passing a law against **quarrying** the Palisades. But the women continued the pressure and in 1900, the Palisades Interstate Park Commission was created to safeguard the cliffs forever.

The Palisades in New Jersey are about 13 miles long and half a mile wide at their widest. They have about 2,500 acres of shoreline along the Hudson River, including the Palisades cliffs.

STEPPING BACK IN TIME

The state capital of Trenton has something to appeal to almost everyone. History is everywhere, from the shimmering State House to the surrounding 19th century homes to Washington Crossing State Park. Right in the downtown area is Mill Hill, a beautiful neighborhood of old row houses. In the 1960s, this part of Trenton was scheduled to be torn down. It was saved by Mayor Arthur Holland, who moved there to prove these historic buildings should be saved. A massive **restoration** effort is still under way. The State Museum, Planetarium, and College of New Jersey are all nearby.

Up the Delaware River toward the New Jersey Highlands is the town of Lambertville. Once a stop on the old railroad line from New York to Philadelphia, the

An Old School

The best-known of the Piedmont's western communities is Princeton. Home to Princeton University—one of the world's most **prestigious** centers of learning—its streets are alive with young people, business people, and artistic people. No other town in New Jersey

is quite like it. Princeton University was established in 1746 as the College of New Jersey. It is one of the oldest colleges in the nation.

The sculpture outside the New Jersey State Museum is El Sol Rojo *by artist Alexander Calder.*

town has always been a **thriving** business center. Today, some of the state's finest art and antiques can be found in this little town. Lambertville's neighbor, Frenchtown, also attracts treasure-hunting tourists.

Many other places in this region of New Jersey are rich in history. In Kingston, a few miles outside of Princeton, you can actually step back into history. A stretch of the old **canal** dug in 1830 to connect Trenton and New Brunswick still exists. Nearby is a stone bridge built in 1798 to replace the one destroyed during the American Revolution (1775–1783). There is also a Presbyterian church in town from the early 1700s.

A few miles east of the Delaware River are the towns of Clinton, Flemington, and Somerville. Clinton's claim to fame is the Clinton Historical Museum Village, which transports visitors to the early 1800s. Clinton is also close to the Round Valley **Recreation** Area, where fishing, boating, and swimming are allowed in the state's deepest lake. In the winter, Round Valley is the site of ice-boat races. Flemington features a complex of

The Clinton Historical Museum was once known as the Red Mill. In the 1800s it produced many goods, including fabric, corn meal, graphite, and talc.

outlet malls which draw bargain hunters from all over the state and even from New York.

Somerville also attracts many people from New York. Some come to the Golf House, which has a collection of **artifacts** and **memorabilia** from the sport. Others come to visit the Cycling Hall of Fame, or to participate in the Tour of Somerville, which is the country's oldest continually run bike race. Duke Gardens is housed in huge greenhouses on the Doris Duke **estate.** The family spent millions of dollars on the gardens in the early 1900s, but they grew food during World War II (1939–1945). Mrs. Duke, who died in 1993, began **restoring** the gardens to their original beauty in the 1960s.

The Duke Gardens are housed in almost an acre of connected greenhouses. There are eleven theme displays that use plants from all over the world.

North of Somerville lie the horse farms and country estates of Bernardsville and Basking Ridge, as well as little towns like Chester. They are just far enough away from the fast-paced **suburbs** to still be considered places for relaxation.

Morristown marks the middle of the Piedmont Plateau region. This city, once at the center of the colonial struggle against Great Britain, marks the unofficial dividing line between the suburbs and the countryside. Morristown itself is more of a city than a suburb. Around its historic village green are sidewalks busy with professionals, families, and shoppers. In and around town are a dozen different museums, parks, and important historical sites, including the Morris Museum, Morristown National Historic Park, and Fosterfield Living Historical Farm.

Roaring Brook

Near Somerville, in the Sourland Mountain Preserve, is one of the state's most interesting natural wonders. During the spring thaw, a little stream called Roaring Brook lives up to its names as it tumbles down the mountainside. In many spots the stream is completely filled with large boulders. As the stream rushes beneath these tightly packed stones, it is **amplified** many times and is quite loud.

*Newark is New Jersey's largest city. It has been an **industrial** area since the late 1800s and early 1900s. Today, Newark is home to over 300 types of businesses.*

27

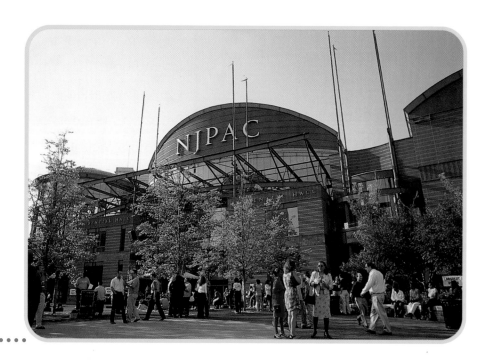

The New Jersey Performing Arts Center opened in 1997. Since then, almost two million people have attended events and performances there.

INDUSTRIAL TOWNS

East of Morristown, toward New York, there are **suburbs** such as Chatham, Summit, Maplewood, and Livingston. They are located outside the old **industrial** areas of New Jersey—cities like Newark, Elizabeth, Bayonne, and Jersey City. Newark is the state's largest city, and one of the oldest major population centers in the United States. It was a major industrial city for more than two centuries, but was hit by hard times in the 1950s. It then became one of the poorest cities on the East Coast.

Newark has had a comeback over the past ten years. It has managed to hold on to the things that once helped it **thrive**—insurance companies, law offices, professional and graduate schools, museums, theaters, a busy **port,** and a growing airport. It has added new attractions, such as the New Jersey Performing Arts Center, Riverfront Stadium, and a complete renovation of both the Newark Museum and the New Jersey Historical Society.

The city of Elizabeth is home to several chemical plants. It was once a beautiful port town, but the elevated New Jersey Turnpike was built through the center of Elizabeth. Bayonne, located on the other side of Newark Bay, is also a center of heavy industry, and has been for more than 100 years. Here, however, stable and attractive working-class neighborhoods have **thrived** for generations, giving Bayonne an energy all its own.

From Jersey City you can see New York City's financial district. The town has become an exciting melting pot of different **cultures** over the last twenty years. As rents in New York and nearby Hoboken have increased in cost, more and more people have moved to Jersey City.

Jersey City has changed greatly over the past twenty years. New businesses and buildings have come to the city, changing the skyline and the city image.

*Today, Hoboken is home to people of many **cultures,** each with its own festivals, languages, music, businesses, and clubs.*

HOBOKEN

Hoboken is a one-mile-square city. Throughout its history it has always been more like a city in New York than one in New Jersey. Hoboken has street after street of brownstone buildings that look like neighborhoods in Manhattan. Hoboken also has one of the finest colleges in the United States, the Stevens Institute of Technology, with more than 3,000 students.

Branch Brook cherry trees

Newark's Branch Brook Park is a 486-acre park between highways and housing projects, with more than 2,000 cherry trees. Each April, they all bloom at once. It is considered the largest cherry blossom display in the world.

BERGEN COUNTY

Bergen County in northeast New Jersey has the state's greatest concentration of people, jobs, and wealth. It is made up of many **suburban** communities. Together, they offer natural beauty, history, shopping, and **industries.** Hackensack, one of the oldest towns in the state, features an old-time business district that has reinvented itself with a mix of old and new stores and restaurants. The Aviation Hall of Fame, which celebrates the history of flying and focuses on the stories of two local boys who became astronauts—Wally Schirra and Edwin "Buzz" Aldrin—is a few minutes south of Hackensack, in Teterboro. Teaneck, across the river, is the county's largest town, with about 50,000 residents, including a very large population of observant and **orthodox** Jews. It is also the home of Fairleigh Dickinson University.

Services **thrive** in Bergen County. The town of Paramus in the eastern part of the county, has five different shopping malls. Ridgewood, a couple of miles north, has become the county's most successful small town, with a business district full of shops and restaurants.

Great Falls is the second-largest waterfall by volume east of the Mississippi River. This means it is not one of the largest in size, but it does contain more water than most.

PASSAIC COUNTY

To the south and west of Bergen County is Passaic County. The city of Paterson, founded in the 1790s by a group led by Alexander Hamilton, is the oldest planned industrial city in the United States. Paterson was built just below the mighty

Great Falls on the Passaic River, which powered its **mills** and factories. Over the centuries, the falls have inspired countless visitors. George Washington marveled at them, while poets William Carlos Williams and Washington Irving wrote about their beauty. To this day, more than 10,000 people a year travel to see the Great Falls. Although Paterson went into a long period of decline, it has always been a strong working-class city. Today, it is a melting pot of new **immigrants,** making it the third-largest city in New Jersey, behind Newark and Jersey City.

Edison's lab in West Orange employed about 60 people. It is said that Edison told new employees, "There ain't no rules around here. We're trying to accomplish something."

South of Paterson and west of Newark, in a **suburban** area that is growing very rapidly, are the towns of West Orange and Montclair. Thomas Edison called

Liberty State Park

Liberty State Park was New Jersey's first **urban** park, and offers great views of and ferries to Ellis Island and the Statue of Liberty. It used to be a busy commuter railroad yard, with more than 25,000 people passing through each day on their way from New Jersey to New York. It was also the place where millions of new immigrants first set foot on the American mainland after being processed at Ellis Island.

West Orange home from 1886 until he died in 1931, and his home and research lab have been preserved as part of a national historic site. West Orange also has a replica of America's first movie studio—another of Edison's countless inventions. In additon, West Orange also boasts much in the way of natural beauty. There are lovely views of New York from the Eagle Rock Reservation, and more than 2,000 acres of parkland in the South Mountain Reservation. A few minutes to the north, Montclair offers a look at one of New Jersey's old-time suburbs, with its grand houses and tree-lined streets. Montclair is a town full of art and music lovers. The Montclair Art Museum is one of New Jersey's very best.

Coastal Plain

New Jersey's Coastal Plain makes up the state's lower half. It stretches south from the mouth of the Raritan River all the way down the Atlantic coast, and from Trenton down to the Delaware Bay. This region, also known as South Jersey, is larger than the other three regions of New Jersey combined. Its eastern edge forms the state's coastline along the Atlantic Ocean. It runs from Sandy Hook all the way south to Cape May, which is the southernmost tip of the state.

The "twin lights" in the Highlands of Navesink were built in 1828. In 1862, they were rebuilt and connected. The lighthouses were named a New Jersey State Historic Site in 1960.

NATURAL RESOURCES

The western part of the Coastal Plain has some of the world's most **fertile** and

productive farmland. New Jersey farmers make more money per acre from their crops than farmers anywhere else in the country.

The Raritan Bay makes up the uppermost part of the Atlantic Coastal Plain. It has easy access to water, excellent fishing, and a wealth of **natural resources.** In the 1600s, settlers used the land for farming. Today, the towns still offer a wide range of opportunities—along with all the other benefits of living near the water.

The Coastal Plain is the largest geographical region in New Jersey. It covers almost one half of the state.

COASTAL PLAIN TOWNS

The largest towns in the Raritan Bay area are New Brunswick and Perth Amboy. New Brunswick, a few miles up the Raritan River, is a busy, **thriving** center of education, **culture,** and **industry.** It is the home of Rutgers University, New Jersey's state college, and its famous art and geology museums, as well as the State Theatre, a popular performing arts center. New Brunswick is known for many things. It was an important stop on the **Underground Railroad,** the birthplace of American football, and home to Johnson & Johnson, creator of the Band-Aid.

Perth Amboy was once the **provincial** capital of New Jersey. For many years it was a busy industrial community, but fell on hard times in the mid-1900s and has never fully recovered.

35

The New Brunswick campus of Rutgers University is the largest of the school's three campuses. About 28,000 students attend school there.

Rumson, on the other hand, has never experienced hard times. Located on a **peninsula** between the Navesink and Shrewsbury Rivers, Rumson is one of the wealthiest communities in the United States. Surrounded on three sides by water, it has been a favorite spot for the rich and famous for more than a century.

Other significant towns in Monmouth County include Freehold, the **county seat,** Colts Neck, known for its horse farms, and Middletown, which has more school children than any other town in the state.

Much of Monmouth County was once farmland. Beginning in the 1950s, when New Yorkers began heading for the **suburbs,** this open space has been taken over by housing. Communities like Matawan, Lincroft, Eatontown, Oakhurst, and Wayside are almost unrecognizable from what they looked like 50 years ago.

ATTRACTIONS

Monmouth County's shore towns make up the northern end of the New Jersey coast, which starts in Sandy Hook and stretches more than 130 miles south along the Atlantic shoreline to Cape May. For centuries, the shifting sands and violent surf caused by Atlantic storms

New Jersey's Hippest Towns

Along the southern shore of Raritan Bay are the towns of Sayreville, Keyport, Keansburg, and Belford. While neighboring communities in Monmouth County underwent a population explosion during the 1970s, 1980s, and 1990s, these bayshore towns were not "discovered" until high-speed ferry service to New York City was started in recent years. Another recently "discovered" Monmouth County town is Red Bank. After years of decline, it has become an **urban oasis** surrounded by wealthy suburbs like Rumson, Locust, Little Silver, Fair Haven, Middletown, Shrewsbury, and Colts Neck. Home of the Count Basie Theater and some of the state's best restaurants, Red Bank now calls itself the "hippest town in New Jersey."

made much of the shore **uninhabitable.** New Jersey's natives and its early European settlers spent little time on these beaches. In the mid 1800s, when Americans had more money and free time, the Jersey shore began to gain popularity as a **resort** area. Several U.S. presidents in the late 1800s spent their summers on the shore, especially in Long Branch and Cape May. This helped make the area even more popular. By the turn of the century, thousands of summer mansions had been constructed near the ocean, hundreds of which still stand today.

People do not live on Sandy Hook, which is known for its famous lighthouse. Just south of Sandy Hook, Ocean Avenue begins. This road continues south through the famous beach towns of Seabright, Long Branch, Elberon, Deal, and Allenhurst, and right into Asbury Park. Asbury, with its long, wide boardwalk, was a summer getaway for nearly a century before becoming rundown during the 1960s and 1970s. In recent years, it has begun a comeback.

South of Asbury are towns such as Ocean Grove, Belmar, and Spring Lake. Walking down the streets of these communities is like stepping back in time. Ocean Grove, founded as a religious community in the 1860s, is world famous for its Great Auditorium, constructed in 1894. An all-wood building with near-perfect **acoustics,** it is the state's largest enclosed auditorium. Spring Lake, once a gathering place for wealthy Irish-Americans, features **restored** homes and has become one of the most popular towns in the state.

Further south along the shore, in Ocean County, is Point Pleasant. Located between Manasquan Inlet and the Metedeconk River, it has something for everyone—a long boardwalk, rides and amusements, seafood restaurants, antique stores and other shopping, and a beach. South of Point Pleasant is a ten-mile-

The Seabright Lawn Tennis and Cricket Club has been open since 1877. Here a woman shows off her trophy from a 1933 tournament win.

long, narrow strip of white sand called Island Beach. This area attracts bird watchers, hikers, swimmers, surfers, scuba divers, and fishing enthusiasts. Island Beach became an island in the 1700s, when the ocean cut it off from the mainland. Before that time, the waters behind it had been a favorite hiding place of pirates and **privateers.**

Ocean County's ultimate vacationer's paradise is further south, on Long Beach Island. This 18-mile-long **barrier island** is within driving distance of New York, Philadelphia, and northern New Jersey. The ocean is unusually cool and clear, the houses range from simple and small to million-dollar mansions, and visitors range from "first-timers" to families that have been summering there for generations. At the northern point of the island is the world-famous Barnegat Lighthouse. "Old Barney" has been the subject of countless paintings and, more than 150 years after going into service, remains one of the most well-built shore structures on the Atlantic coast.

The current Great Auditorium was built in 1894. It is almost the size of a football field. There are free organ concerts on Wednesdays and Saturdays and church services on Sundays.

The next major stop on the Jersey Shore is Atlantic City. Once the nation's most celebrated beach **resort,** the town fell into steep decline after World War II (1939–1945). Atlantic City is a popular place again today, thanks to the thirteen large casinos located there.

Between Atlantic City and Cape May are more barrier-island resorts, including Ocean City and the Wildwoods.

Cape May

Cape May, located at the southern tip of New Jersey, has been a popular **resort** since before the Civil War (1861–1865). Today, the entire town is a national historic landmark. Cape May has some of the finest examples of Victorian buildings, with decorative woodwork and attention to detail. Many of the old homes have been painted with bright colors—a tradition started in the 1800s to make the homes stand out in the fog. They have been nicknamed "Painted Ladies."

Ocean City's three-mile boardwalk makes it a popular family vacation spot. The Wildwoods include three separate towns: Wildwood, Wildwood Crest, and North Wildwood. Wildwood is best known for its three great amusement piers and extremely wide beaches. Wildwood Crest has some of New Jersey's last "funky 50s" motels. North Wildwood is best known for its Hereford Inlet Lighthouse, constructed in 1874.

MORE ATTRACTIONS

The southwestern part of New Jersey is as different from the shore as it is from the northern counties. Along the shoreline where the Delaware River widens into Delaware Bay are the **rural** areas of Cumberland and Salem Counties. History lovers are drawn to Bridgeton, the central point of a district that has over

Barnegat Lighthouse is the second-tallest lighthouse in the United States. It has not been used since 1944, but people still come to visit the lighthouse every year.

2,200 important buildings and old homes. It is the state's largest historic district. Among the more popular stops is the Sweden Farmstead Museum, a replica of a 1600s farm run by the colony's Swedish settlers. The nearby Cohanzick Zoo has many rare animals, including a white tiger.

The other large town in this part of New Jersey is the **port** city of Salem. Heavy **industry** never came to this area, so much of Salem's 1800s charm remains intact. One of the state's few pre-colonial trees stands on the grounds of the First Presbyterian Church. Known as the Salem Oak, it dates back well over 400 years and is considered so important that its branches and acorns are plucked off the ground soon after they fall and are preserved. Salem was the center of American glassblowing in the mid-1700s. The business later shifted a few miles north and east when seven brothers from a German glassblowing family decided to start their own business nearer to the Pinelands. The Pinelands provided a steady supply of wood to fuel their furnaces. Today, this place is known as Glassboro. Just

There is more to do in Atlantic City than just go to the casinos. The beach, boardwalk, museums, water parks, historic buildings, and shops are all available for tourists to enjoy.

north of Salem, along the Delaware River, is one of southern New Jersey's few surviving military structures from the 1800s, Fort Mott. Further up the river, in Gloucester County, is the Red Bank Battlefield. This park marks the site of a key battle in the early days of the American Revolution (1775–1783).

INDUSTRY

Further up the Delaware River is Camden, southern New Jersey's major **urban** area. It lies right across the river from Philadelphia, and was once a center of shipping and **industry.** Like many river towns, Camden's **economy** suffered when ways other than water were created to move manufactured goods. After a long period of decay, however, it has begun to rebuild. Camden has been transformed by the development of the city's waterfront, a 25,000-seat **amphitheater,** an aquarium, and the rebuilding of its neighborhoods. Its well-off **suburbs** of Cherry Hill, Haddonfield, and Mt.

Wildwood has the tallest Ferris wheel on the east coast. "The Great Nor'Easter" is a suspended looping rollercoaster of which there are only four in the world.

Pine Barrens

Although the Atlantic Shore is New Jersey's most popular destination, for nature-lovers nothing can match the area just a few miles inland, called the Pinelands, or Pine Barrens. It covers more than 2,000 square miles and touches as many as seven different counties. This area is a unique **ecosystem** of sandy soil, scrub pine, and rare plant and animal **species.** It is also very sensitive to human contact, so much of the area has been protected by the government.

There are few houses within New Jersey's Pinelands area. The largest town within the Pine Barrens is Chatsworth, with a population only in the hundreds. Most of the towns in this part of the state grew up along the forest's fringes, including Tom's River to the east, Hammonton to the west, and Woodbine to the south. Also in this area are two military bases, Fort Dix and McGuire Air Force Base. The most historic communities in the area are Millville—site of America's first Native American **reservation** and home to the glassblowing museum at Wheaton Village—and Vineland, which attracted some of the state's first Italian **immigrants.** Today, more New Jerseyans trace their roots back to Italy than any other country.

Laurel mean that there is plenty of money that can be brought back downtown as things improve. Haddonfield is noteworthy for its Indian King Tavern. It was in this building that members of the Assembly met to pass **legislation** in 1777 that officially made New Jersey a state. It was also a stop on the **Underground Railroad.**

Almost all of the towns in New Jersey's Atlantic Coastal Plain have experienced explosive growth in recent years.

The Camden waterfront shares the Delaware River banks with Penn's Landing, just one mile from Philadelphia's historic district.

However, few can claim to have undergone a transformation like the one taking place along Interstate 95. This area where Ocean County meets Monmouth County thirty miles west of the Atlantic Ocean used to be a near-deserted stretch of land. Home buyers looking for open, affordable land began trickling into the area during the 1970s. Today, that trickle is a flood of people. This area is close to three of the state's major highways—which makes commuting to work easy—and is a short drive to the Atlantic beaches. It is also the home of the Six Flags amusement park complex, and Allaire State Park, which has an old New Jersey village, and an operating steam locomotive.

THIS IS NEW JERSEY

New Jersey may be one of the smallest states in the nation, but it is one of the busiest and most productive. People of all races and **cultures** call New Jersey home. **Industries** develop and sell new products. Tourists visit the casinos and beaches. Highways, railroads, and airports connect people to all parts of the world. From the remote areas near the Applachian Mountains to the busy cities of Newark, Trenton, and Atlantic City, New Jersey has something to offer everyone.

Map of New Jersey

Glossary

acoustic related to the hearing of sound

amplified made louder than normal

amphitheater oval or circular building used for concerts and other large events

artifact something created by humans for a practical purpose during a certain time period

artificial not real

barrier island long island that protects the shore from the effects of the ocean

canal man-made waterway for boats

climate weather conditions that are usual for a certain area

conservationist person involved in the planned management of natural resources to prevent waste, destruction, or neglect

county seat town that handles county administration

culture ideas, skills, arts, and a way of life of a certain people at a certain time

densely crowded together

dormant temporarily inactive

economy means of bringing money to a region

ecosystem community of living things, together with the environment in which they live

estate fine country house on a large piece of land

fertile bearing crops or vegetation in abundance

geologist scientist who studies the history of the earth through rocks

gorge narrow steep-walled canyon or part of a canyon

gross state product value of the total amount of goods and services produced by the people of a state during a certain time

high-tech having to do with technology and computers. High-tech is the shortened form of high technology

immigrant one who moves to another country to settle

industry group of businesses that offer a similar product or service

landform natural feature of a land surface

legislation laws

memorabilia something that serves as a reminder

mill building with machinery for grinding grain into flour

natural resource something from nature that is available to take care of a need

oasis something that provides refuge and relief

ore rock or mineral from which a metal can be obtained

orthodox holding established beliefs, especially in religion

peninsula piece of land extending over a body of water

pharmaceutical having to do with medication

port place where ships load and unload cargo

prestigious important in the eyes of the people

privateer armed private ship that attacks enemy shipping

promenade place for walking

provincial time when New Jersey was governed by Great Britain

quaint pleasingly or strikingly old-fashioned

quarrying taking useful material from stone

recreation means of refreshing the mind and body

refuge shelter or protection from distress

reservation public land set aside for use by Native Americans

resort place providing recreation and entertainment, especially to vacationers

restore bring back to an original state

rural having to do with the country or farmland

scenic of or relating to natural scenery

secluded screened or hidden from view

species group of organisms that share the same physical characteristics

suburb city or town just outside a larger city

temperate not extreme or excessive

thriving doing very well

topographical how high or low the elevation of land is

Underground Railroad system of cooperation by antislavery people in the United States before 1863 by which runaway slaves were secretly helped to reach freedom

uninhabitable unable to be lived in

urban relating to the city

vista distant view through or along an avenue or opening

More Books to Read

Kummer, Patricia K. *New Jersey*. Minnetonka, Minn.: Bridgestone Books, 1998.

Moragne, Wendy. *New Jersey*. Tarrytown, N.Y.: Benchmark Books, 2000.

Scholl, Elizabeth. *New Jersey*. San Francisco: Children's Book Press, 2002.

Stein, R. Conrad and Deborah Ken. *New Jersey*. Danbury, Conn.: Children's Press, 1998.

Welsbacher, Anne. *New Jersey*. Edina, Minn.: Checkerboard Library, 1998.

Index

About the Author

Mark Stewart makes his home in New Jersey. A graduate of Duke University with a degree in history, Stewart has authored more than 100 nonfiction titles for the school and library market. He and his wife Sarah have two daughters, Mariah and Rachel.

ABA-5846